Gateways
to Science

Gateways to Science

Neal J. Holmes
Department of Chemistry
Coordinator of Science Education
Central Missouri State University

John B. Leake
Department of Science Education
University of Missouri

Mary W. Shaw
Department of Education
Montgomery County, Maryland

Webster Division, McGraw-Hill Book Company
New York/St. Louis/Dallas/San Francisco/Auckland/Bogotá/Guatemala
Hamburg/Johannesburg/Lisbon/London/Madrid/Mexico/Montreal/New Delhi
Panama/Paris/San Juan/São Paulo/Singapore/Sydney/Tokyo/Toronto

This book was set in 18 point Aster by Black Dot. The color separation was done by Black Dot

 2 3 4 5 6 7 8 9 10 DODO 93 92 91 90 89 88 87 86 85 84

ISBN 0-07-029910-2

Consultants and Reviewers

Alden Loomis   Montebello Unified School District, Montebello, California

Patricia F. Erikson   Ryan Road School, Northampton, Massachusetts

Dr. John P. Huntsberger   Science Education Center, The University of Texas at Austin, Austin, Texas

Dr. Charles J. LaRue   Montgomery County Schools, Rockville, Maryland

Miriam R. Buckland   K.T. Murphy School, Stamford, Connecticut

Joseph T. Piazza   Easton Area School District, Easton, Pennsylvania

James E. Williamson   Lamar Junior High School, Irving, Texas

Alice Kimbler Hankla   The Galloway School, Atlanta, Georgia

Saralee Semon   School Four, Fort Lee, New Jersey

Dr. Floyd D. Ploeger   Southwest Educational Development Laboratory, Austin, Texas

Editor in Chief: John F. Mongillo
Sponsoring Editor: Dennis Colella
Editorial Assistant: Helga Rauch

Manchester Publishing Unit
Project Leader: Neysa Chouteau
Editing and Styling: Robert Towns
Design and Art Supervision: Virginia Copeland
Production: Tom Goodwin
Editorial Assistant: Frieda Amiri

Associate Editor: Jane O'Connor
Photo Researcher: Randy Matusow
Cover Photo Research: Alan Forman
Text and Cover Design: Group Four, Inc.
Cover Photo: M. Newman/The Image Bank
Layout and Art Production: Cover to Cover, Inc.
Artist: Roberta Collier
Contributing Writers: Mary Hicks, Barbara Branca

Contents

Life science

Earth and space science

Physical science

Life science

Health and safety

1

Dandelions

What is growing in the **field**?

Find a **dandelion**.

3

Find a dandelion **flower**.

What color is it?

Find a dandelion **leaf**.

What color is it?

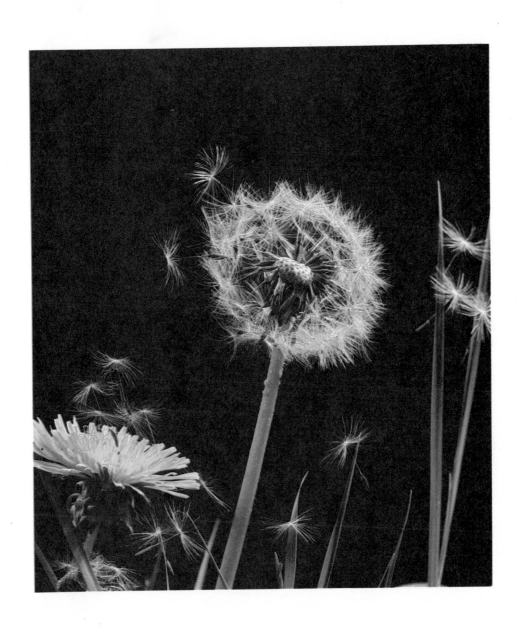

Find some dandelion **seeds**.

Where are the seeds?

What color is a seed?

Blow on some dandelion seeds.
Where will they go?

Dandelions change.

What changes do you see?

Activity

Draw a plant

Draw a dandelion.

Color it.

Name the flower, leaf, and seeds.

Write the names on the drawing.

Show what you know

Look at the flowers.

Find the dandelions.

Stems and roots

Dig up a plant.

Part grows under the ground.

It is called the **root**.

Part grows above the ground.

It is called the **stem.**

Leaves also grow above ground.

Stem

Leaves

Root

Most plants have stems and roots.

Find some stems.

Find some roots.

People eat the stems of some plants.

People eat the roots of some plants.

Animals eat stems and roots, too.

Vegetables are stems and roots.

They are also flowers and leaves we eat.

Can you name these vegetables?

Activity

Make a chart

Make a vegetable chart.

Look for pictures of stems and roots.

Cut them out.

Paste the pictures on the chart.

Which ones do you like?

Stems We Eat	Roots We Eat
celery	carrots
asparagus	beets

Show what you know

Look at these vegetables.

Which are roots?

Which are stems?

Which are leaves?

17

3

Seeds

This is an **oak** tree.

An oak tree has **seeds.**

The seeds are **acorns**.

Many acorns fall from an oak.

What happens to these seeds?

Will all acorns grow into oaks?

20

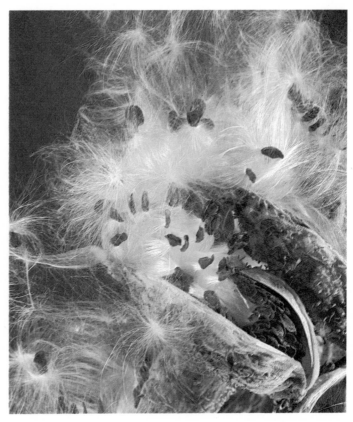

Some seeds **grow** where they fall.

Other seeds stick to animals.

And then the seeds drop off the animals.

Birds carry away seeds.

Wind carries seeds to other places.

Water carries away seeds, as well.

Many plants grow from seeds.

Look **inside** a seed.
What do you see?

Activity

Plant a seed

Plant a **bean** seed.

Watch it grow.

How does it change?

Here are some seeds.

Which seeds can we eat?

Show what you know

Make a plant and seed chart.

Leaves

These are **maple** leaves.

They come from a maple tree.

These **pine needles** are leaves, too.
What tree do they come from?

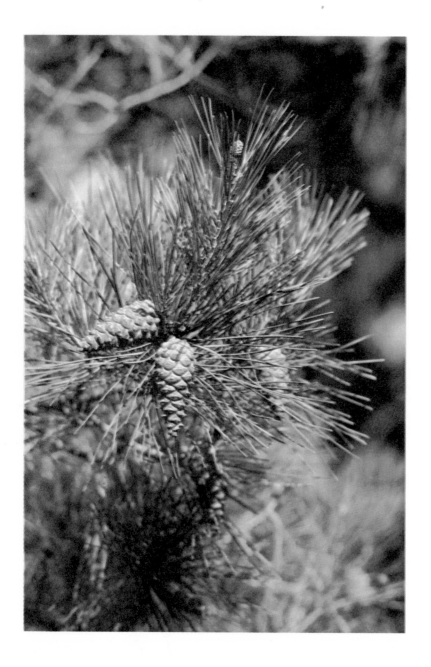

Find some leaves.

Fold the leaves in **half.**

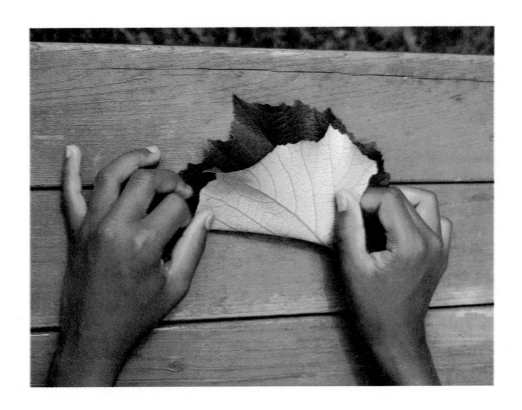

Do both sides of a leaf match?

Activity

Make a half leaf whole

Cut a leaf in half.

Put a mirror along the cut side.

Look in the mirror.

What do you see?

Show what you know

Match each leaf with its tree.

5

Buds

Buds tell us a plant is living.

Leaves grow from buds.

Flowers grow from buds, too.

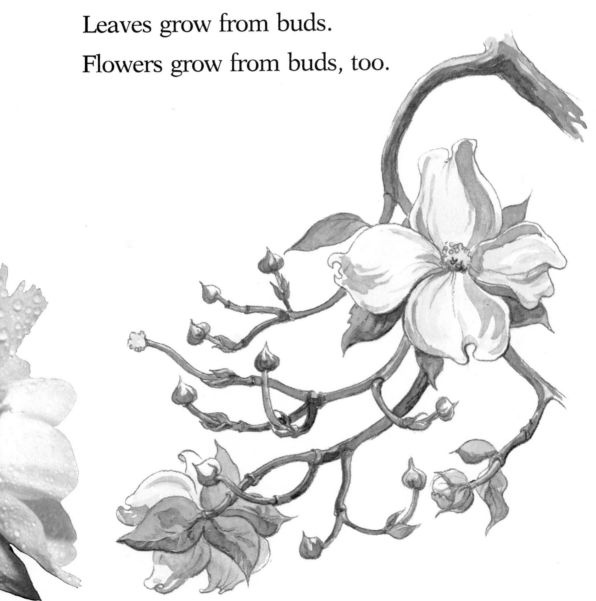

This is a bud on a **branch**.

This is the bud 1 week **later**.

This is the bud 2 weeks later.

This is the bud 3 weeks later.

Was this a flower bud?
Was it a leaf bud?

Look at the **pussy willow** buds.

These buds are flower buds.

Pussy willows are **gray** flowers.

Look at the **lilac** buds.

What will grow from them?

What makes buds open?

Buds need water and warm air.

Then they will open.

Most buds open in spring.

Not all buds grow in spring.

Some plants grow flower buds in fall.

House plants grow leaf buds all year.

Activity

Make buds open

Most buds open in spring.

Make some buds open **earlier**.

Bring them inside.

Put them in water.

Watch them open.

Show what you know

Which sentences are right?

1. Buds grow into plant parts.

2. Buds are always on branches.

3. A bud can become a leaf or a flower.

4. Buds grow only in spring.

6

Goldfish

Watch a **goldfish**.

What color is it?

Goldfish are like most fish.

They live in water.

They use **fins** to **swim**.

Find the fins on this fish.

Many fish have a long tail.

Most fish have **scales**.

Look at the goldfish.

Can you see its scales?

Does it have a long tail?

How does a goldfish use its tail?

Look at this fish.

It has a good shape for swimming.

Why is the bottom side light?

It is easy to care for a goldfish.

Activity

Make an aquarium

Put water in a jar.

Put a water plant in the jar.

Add a goldfish.

Feed your fish every day.

Show what you know

Which sentences are right?

1. Goldfish live in water.

2. Goldfish use their fins to eat.

3. Only goldfish have scales.

4. The bottom side of a goldfish is light.

Animal life

Most animals move around.

Many water animals use fins.

Most land animals use legs.

Most birds **travel** in the air.

They use their wings to fly.

How do **snakes** move?

Animals **escape danger** in many ways.

Birds fly away.

A **chipmunk** can run away to escape.

It can also hide in its hole.

This **stonefish** escapes danger.

It looks like a rock.

Activity

How do animals escape danger?

Look at each picture.

How does a turtle escape danger?

How does this rabbit escape danger?

How do these zebras escape danger?

Animals get food in many ways.

Many animals eat other animals.

Birds have **sharp beaks.**

Some birds can catch bugs.

An **anteater** has a long **tongue.**

Its tongue is sticky, too.

So this animal can catch tiny ants.

Many animals do not catch food.

Their food does not run away.

What kind of food is this?

What animals eat this food?

Show what you know

Look at each picture.

How is the animal like an animal you know?

1. This animal moves most like
   a _____ .
   turtle   chipmunk   robin

2. This animal escapes danger most
   like a _____ .
   stonefish   chipmunk   cat

3. This animal gets food most like
   a _____ .
   bird   deer   dog

Ocean life

An **ocean** is very wide.

You cannot see land across an ocean.

An ocean is full of **salt** water.

An ocean is full of living things.

What lives in an ocean?

Plants grow in the ocean.

One ocean plant is called **seaweed**.

What color is seaweed?

Animals live in the ocean, too.

Some ocean animals are very small.

Some ocean animals are very large.

Some **whales** are 30 meters (100 feet) long!

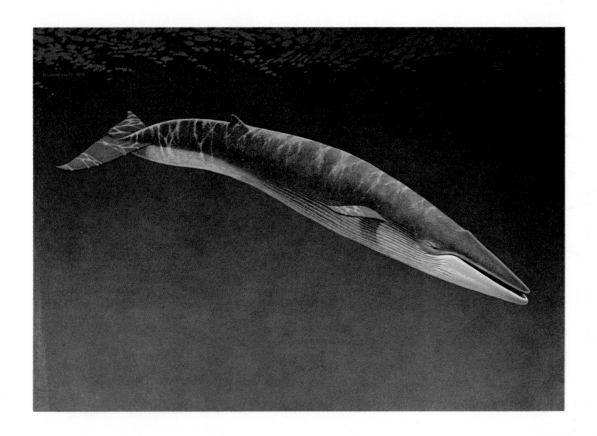

Many animals live in the ocean.

This is a **seashore**.

This is where the ocean and land meet.

What can you find at a seashore?

Some animals live in **shells**.

You can find shells in the sand.

Look for other things.

Activity

Make an ocean picture

Make a class picture.

Paint a big ocean and seashore.

Draw a plant or an animal.

Color it. Cut it out.

Paste it on the class picture.

Show what you know

Which sentences are right?

1. A whale is very small.

2. Seaweed is an ocean plant.

3. Some animals have shells.

4. Ocean and land meet at the seashore.

9

Tracks

Animals make tracks.

Tracks show which way the animal went.

A deer makes tracks in the snow.

Which way is the deer going?

A mouse makes little tracks.

Find its tracks in the snow.

Find its **tail** track.

Big animals make big tracks.

A horse is big.

Find its tracks in the snow.

Are they big?

A **fox** makes tracks in the snow.

The fox came near the horse's tracks.

Find the fox's tracks.

Are they as big as the horse's tracks?

Many things make tracks.

We can find tracks in snow.

We can find them in wet sand.

We can find them on a **sidewalk**.

We can even find them in our homes.

What made these tracks?

Activity

Make some tracks

See how tracks are made.

Get some small things.

Press them into clay.

Take them out.

Look at the clay.

What do you see?

Show the clay to a friend.

Guess what made the track.

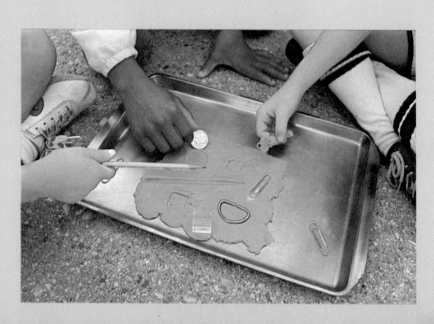

Find some animal tracks.

All animal tracks are not the same.

How are they **different**?

Show what you know

What made these tracks?

10

Senses

We have five **senses**.

They help us find out about things.

We see things with our **eyes**.

We see animals.

We see colors.

We see boys and girls.

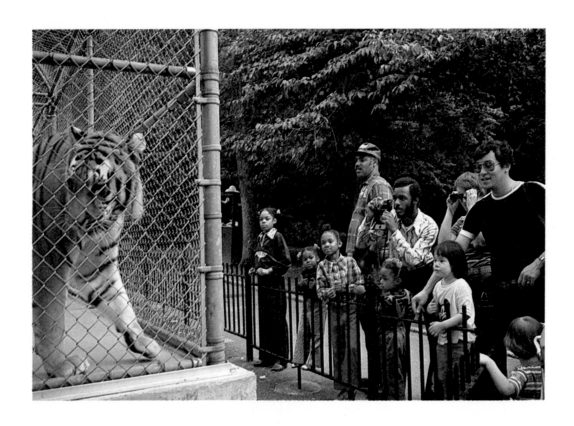

What can you see here?

You **taste** things with your **tongue**.

You **smell** things with your nose.

What can you taste and smell?

Have a party, and see!

We hear things with our **ears**.

Play a game.

What do you hear?

We **feel** things with our **skin**.

A kitten feels **soft**.

Ice feels cold.

How does water feel?

Activity

Play a game

Put some things in a bag.

Ask a friend to touch one thing.

Ask how it feels.

Ask what it is.

Show what you know

Make a chart about your five senses.

We see.		
We hear.		
We smell.		
We taste.		
We feel.		

11

Feeling good

What do we need to stay **healthy**?

Can you think of some things?

Everyone needs food to stay healthy.

Milk and fruit are good for us.

Fish, meat, and bread are good, too.

Here are some good foods.

Name some good foods that you eat.

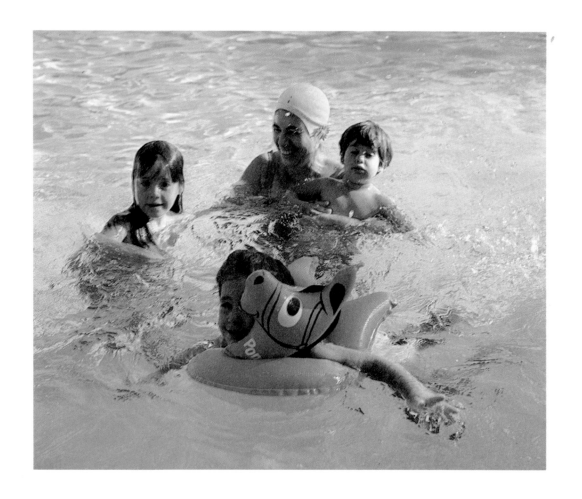

We need to **exercise** every day.

Swimming is fun.

It is one way to exercise.

Can you think of some other ways?

We get tired from work.

We get tired from play, too.

Rest and sleep help us **feel** well.

Rest and sleep help us stay healthy.

Activity

Make a clock

Make a cardboard clock.

Color the clock.

Color the numbers.

Show the time you go to sleep.

Show the time you wake up.

How many hours do you sleep?

Staying **clean** is good for us.

We wash our face and hands.

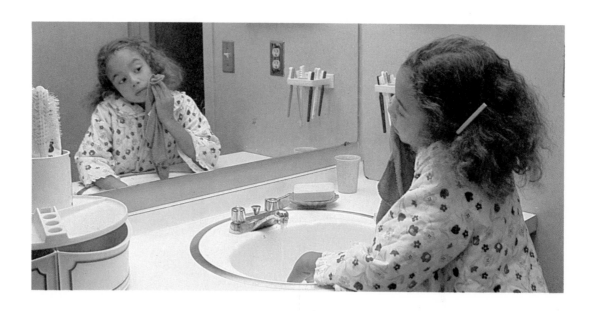

We brush our teeth.

This helps us stay healthy.

The doctor helps us stay healthy, too.
Visit the doctor for a **checkup**.

Show what you know

How do you stay healthy?

Draw a picture.

Tell what you do.

12

Safety for you

Do you walk to school?

Do you ride a bus to school?

Do you walk, ride, and play **safely**?

Here are some things to think about.

Streets are for cars, trucks, and buses.

Sidewalks are for people.

Walk on the sidewalk to be safe.

You want to cross the street.

This boy shows you how.

He walks to the corner.

He crosses only at **crossings**.

Be sure the light for you is green.

Be sure the sign says WALK.

Look both ways for cars.

Do you ride the bus safely?

Sit in your seat, and talk **softly**.

The playground is a place for fun.

But sometimes we are not **careful.**

We can get hurt.

Activity

Playing safely

What do you do in the playground?

Make a list like this one.

Think of ways you can play safely.

Add other things to your list.

Things I Do	Ways of playing safely
swings	Don't swing too high.
slide	
seesaw	

Show what you know

Here are some things to think about:

1. You want to cross the street.
   What should you do?

2. You are riding the bus.
   How should you ride?

3. You are playing on the swing.
   How should you swing?

space science

13

Temperature

What is the **temperature**?

Is it hot?

Is it cold?

How can you tell?

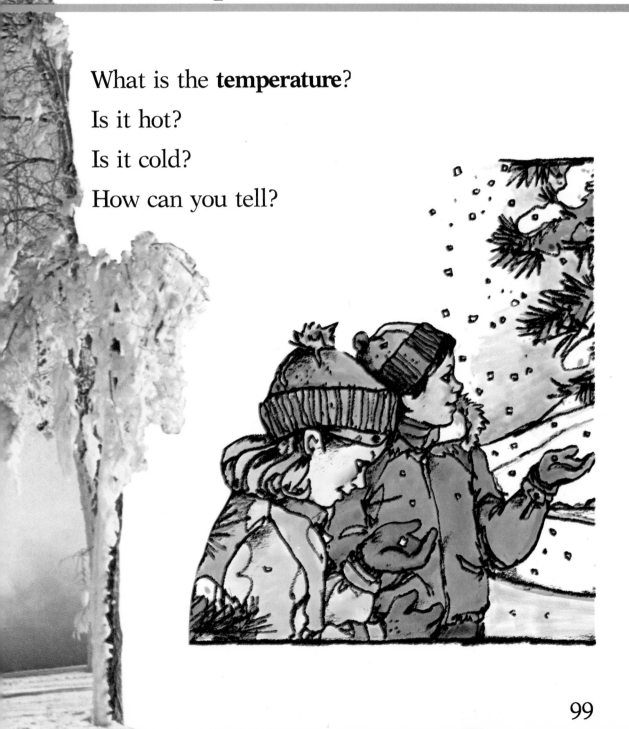

Look at a **thermometer**.

A thermometer tells if it is hot or cold.

A thermometer **measures** temperature.

Red **liquid** can move up or down.

The temperature gets colder.

The liquid moves down.

The temperature gets warmer.

The liquid moves up.

Activity

Look out the window

Look out your window.

What do you see?

Is it rainy or sunny?

Is it snowing?

Draw the way the sky looks.

Is it hot or cold outside?

Find the temperature.

Write it on your picture.

People wear light clothes in hot **weather**.

Some people swim.

Some people lie in the sun.

What do you do when it is hot?

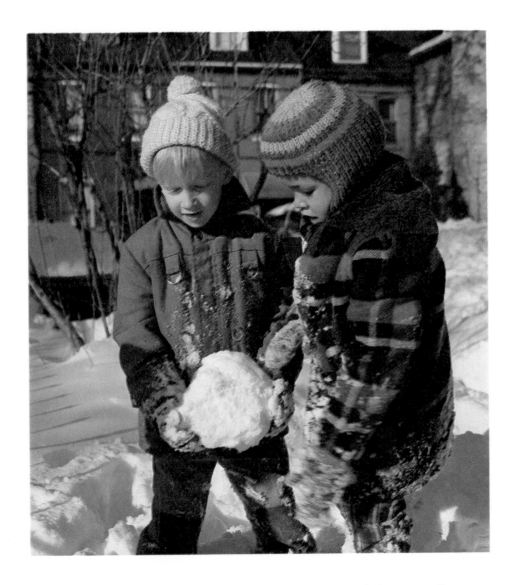

People wear warm clothes in cold weather.

Some people skate.

Some people play in the snow.

What do you do when it is cold?

Some things make the temperature change.

A fireplace can make things warm.

A fan can make things cool.

What makes your home warm or cool?

Show what you know

Make a calendar.

Show the temperature for each day.

Draw pictures to show the weather.

14

Water in air

Water is all around us.

Clouds are made of water.

The water comes from the **air.**

How does water get into the air?

After rain, find a puddle.

How big is the puddle?

Wait for the sun.

Look at the puddle.

How big is it now?

How long will it stay?

What do you see?

What is happening to the puddle?

Make a chart.

Write down what you see.

Time	Size	Deep	Wide
9:00 a.m.			
11:00 a.m.			
1:00 p.m.			
3:00 p.m.			

Activity

Where does water go?

Put some water on a towel.

See where the water goes.

Wait.

Look again.

Is the towel still **wet**?

Where did the water go?

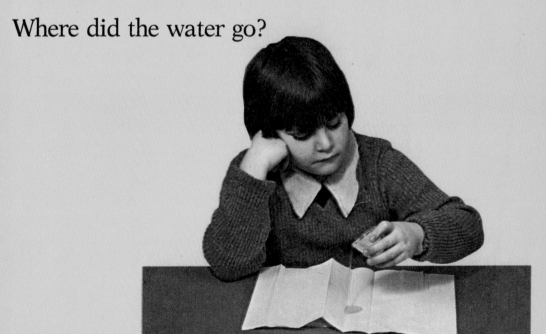

Look at the hot water.

What is happening?

Where is the water going?

Heat helps water get into the air.

Hot air can hold lots of water.

Take three wet mittens.

Put one in the sun.

Shake one mitten.

Leave one mitten alone.

Which **dries** first?

Which dries last?

Show what you know

Which sentences are right?

1. Water is in the air all the time.

2. Heat makes things dry slowly.

3. The sun makes a puddle grow bigger.

4. Water from wet things goes into the air.

15

Day and night

In **daytime**, it is light out.

The sun gives us light.

It is easy to see things.

We can see flowers and water.

Sometimes we can see the sun.

What can you see in the daytime?

It is **dark** at night.

The sun is gone.

It is not easy to see at night.

Sometimes we can see the **moon**.

Sometimes we can see **stars**.

What can you see at night?

One **whole** day has day and night.

Daytime begins when the sun **rises**.

What do people do in the daytime?

In the evening, the sun sets.

It is now night.

What do people do at nighttime?

After nighttime, daytime comes again.

Activity

Make a chart

What do you do in the daytime?

What do you do at nighttime?

Make a list like this one.

Write a check (✔) for daytime.

Or write a check (✔) for nighttime.

Add other things to your list.

Things I Do	Daytime	Night
1. I eat lunch.		
2. I play with my friends.		
3. I take a bath.		

We see and hear things in the day.

We see and hear things at night.

What things tell us it is day?

What things tell us it is night?

Show what you know

These are pictures from one day.

What is the first thing you do?

Then what will you do?

What is the last thing you do?

16

Seasons

There are four **seasons** in a year.

Can you name them?

Winter

In many places, **winter** is very cold.

The days are short.

The nights are long.

Winter may bring snow and ice.

Winter may bring a lot of rain.

What is winter like where you live?

Spring

The days get warmer in **spring**.

In many places, buds grow on trees.

Birds make nests in spring.

What do you do in spring?

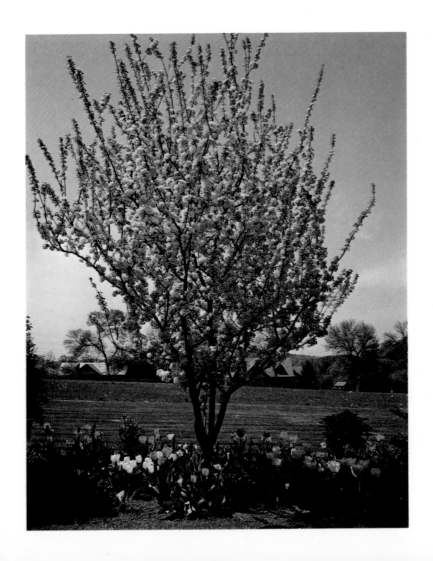

Summer

In many places, **summer** is very hot.

The days are long.

The nights are short.

Some people pick flowers.

Some people go swimming.

What is summer like where you live?

Fall

Fall comes after summer.

In some places, leaves change color.

Days get colder.

Animals get ready for winter.

What do you do in fall?

Activity

Name the Seasons

Look at each picture.

Match each season to a picture.

How did you know?

Show what you know

Make a seasons chart.

Season	People	Plants	Animals
Winter			
Spring			
Summer			
Fall			

3

Physical science

Mirrors

What is a **mirror**?

A mirror is **shiny**.

You can see yourself in a mirror.

Sometimes a **window** is a mirror.

It is **dark** outside the window.

There is light in front of the window.

You can see yourself in the window.

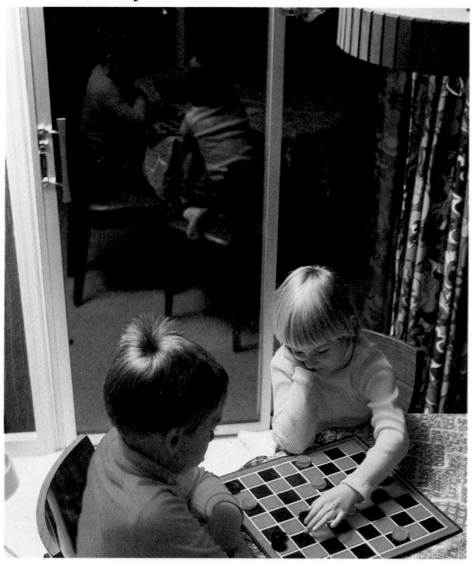

Water can be a mirror.

A puddle is a little mirror.

A lake is a big mirror.

When is water a good mirror?

Hold a book.

Look in a mirror.

What do you see?

Does the book look the same?

A mirror can make things look **backward**.

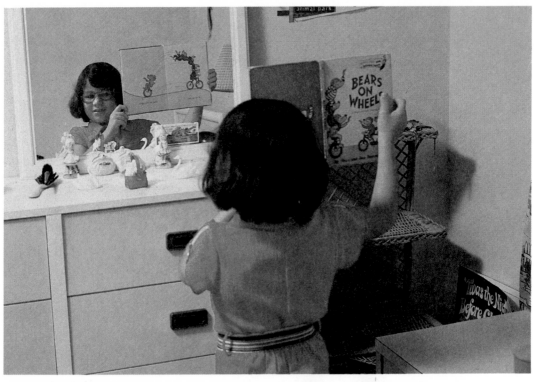

Use a mirror.

Make this look backward.

HO

A mirror can make things look **whole**.

A mirror can make the bread look whole.

Activity

Working with mirrors

Look at these pictures in a mirror.

How does each picture look?

Show what you know

Which sentences are right?

1. A mirror is shiny.

2. A window is always a mirror.

3. Sometimes water is a mirror.

4. A mirror makes things look backward.

Shadows

Here are some **shadows**.

What things are making the shadows?

Can the shadows help you guess?

How are shadows made?

You need **bright** light.

You need something to **block** the light.

People and animals can make shadows.

Houses can make shadows.

Windows do not make shadows.

They do not block the light.

Look at these shadows.

What is blocking the light?

Activity

Does a shadow move?

Make your own shadow.

Have a friend draw around it.

Move away.

Look at your shadow drawing.

Where is your shadow now?

Why did it move?

Sometimes you see shadows.

Sometimes you do not.

Why do shadows go away?

We can use shadows to tell time.

Where is the shadow in the **morning**?

Where is the shadow at **noon**?

Where is the shadow in the **afternoon**?

Show what you know

1. Be a shadow maker.

    Make some shadows.

    What is blocking the light?

    Have your friends guess.

2. Make a little shadow grow.

    Make a shadow with your hand.

    Make the shadow bigger.

Simple machines

Susan's wagon is full of pumpkins.

The wagon has **wheels.**

The wheels make pulling the wagon easy.

Wheels are simple **machines.**

Roger is carrying his pumpkins.

Who is using a machine to move pumpkins?

The box is too heavy to lift.

Mr. Chan can use a **ramp.**

A ramp makes lifting easy.

Mr. Chan pushes the box up the ramp.

A long ramp makes lifting even easier.

Is a ramp a machine?

Carole cuts her birthday cake with a knife.

One side of the knife is sharp.

Careful, Carole!

The other side is dull.

A knife is a **wedge.**

We use a wedge to cut things.

A wedge is a machine, too.

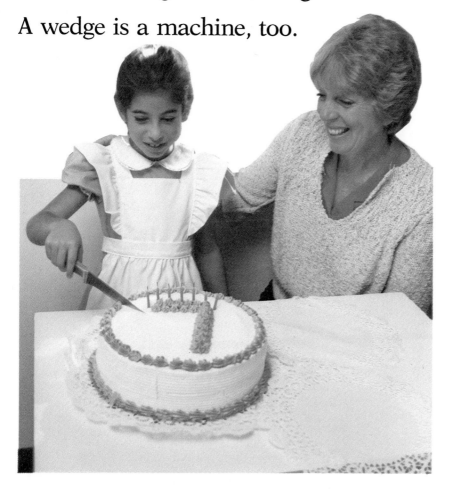

Mark is pushing down on the seesaw.

Steve goes up into the air.

A seesaw is a **lever.**

A lever is a simple machine.

It lifts something up when you push down.

Activity

Make a lever

Put your book at the end of a table.

Put a ruler under the book.

Press down on the ruler.

See what happens to the book.

Can a ruler be a lever?

A machine makes work easier to do.

Machines can work together.

Look at the picture.

What machines are working together?

Show what you know

Match the machine with its job.

A lever lifts things.

A ramp lifts things, too.

A wedge cuts things.

A wheel turns things.

20

Magnets

What can we learn about **magnets**?

Some of these things **stick** to a magnet.

Some do not.

What will a magnet pick up?

A magnet will pick up a pin.

A magnet will pick up a **nail**.

Will a magnet pick up paper?

Try it, and see.

Activity

What can magnets do?

Put two magnets near each other.

What happens?

Magnets can **push away** from each other.

Magnets can **pull towards** each other.

Can one magnet pick up another?

Try it, and see.

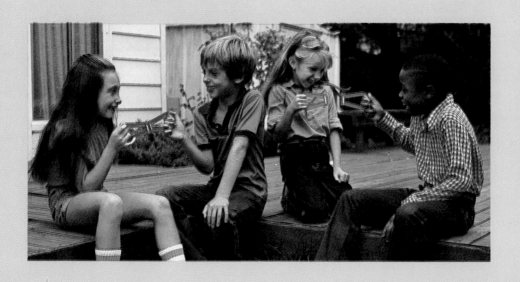

Magnets have different names.

Their shape tells their name.

Find a **horseshoe** magnet.

Find a bar magnet.

Find a ring magnet.

People use magnet **power**.

Look for magnets.

Magnets help people at work.

Magnets help people at school.

Magnets help people at home.

Do magnets help you?

Show what you know

What can a magnet pick up?

Find things in your classroom.

Make a chart.

Objects		Yes	No
1.	paper clip	✓	
2.	key		
3.	tacks		
4.	chalk		
5.			

21

A closer look

Find a **leaf**.

Look at it **closely**.

What can you see?

Look at the same leaf.

Use a **magnifying glass**.

What can you see now?

Look at some sand.

Each **grain** of sand was part of a rock.

What color are the grains of sand?

Look at other little things.

Use a magnifying glass.

Little things look bigger.

Activity

Take a closer look

Look closely at some **sugar**.

Draw what you see.

Look at the sugar again.

Use a magnifying glass.

Draw what you see.

Does the magnifying glass help you?

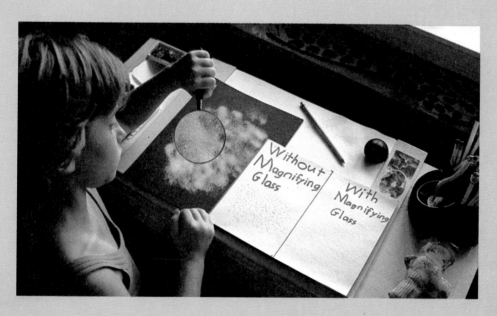

Look at other things.

Look at a quarter.

Look at your hand.

Use a magnifying glass.

See things you could not see before.

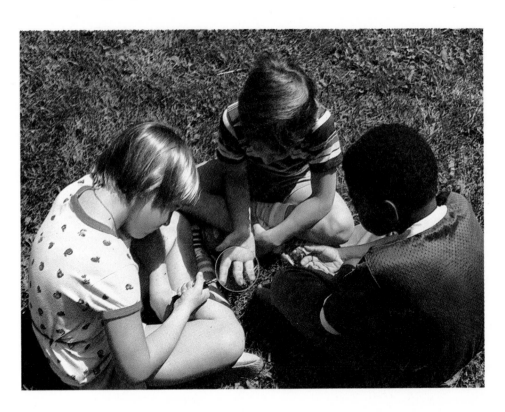

Find a **newspaper**.

Find a page with a picture.

Look at the picture.

Use a magnifying glass.

What did you find out?

Show what you know

What is it?

Match the word with the picture.

Leaf

Sand

Coin

Newspaper Picture

Discover more

You can learn more about your world.

Ask your mom or dad to help.

Look at the animal.

Take good care of the animal.

1. Be sure it has food.

2. Be sure it is not too hot or too cold.

3. Be sure it has a clean home.

Grow plants.

You need: seeds   water

                soil   sunshine

                      pot

Find leaves, shells, or rocks.

Write down what you see and find.

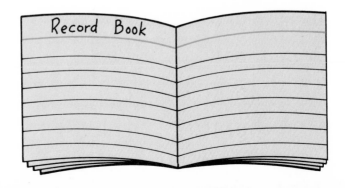

Record Book

Vocabulary/Index

Picture credits

1: Kent & Donna Dannen; **2:** Yeager & Kay/Photo Researchers; **4:** Grant Heilman Photography; **5:** Jane Burton/Bruce Coleman, Inc; **6t:** Roberta Collier, **6b:** Frank Siteman/Stock, Boston; **7tl:** Hans Pfletschinger/Peter Arnold, Inc, **7cl:** S. J. Krasemann/Peter Arnold, Inc.; **7cr:** Brian Milne/Earth Scenes, **7b:** Ken Brate/Photo Researchers; **8:** Robert Capece/McGraw-Hill; **9tl:** S. H. Gottscho/American Museum of Natural History, **9tr:** Grant Heilman Photography, **9bl:** J. E. Thompson/American Museum of Natural History, **9bc:** Barbara Pfeffer/Peter Arnold, Inc., **9br:** Richard Weiss/Peter Arnold, Inc.;

10: Peter Vadnai/McGraw-Hill; **13tl:** A.Singer/Phototake, **13br:** Grant Heilman Photography; **14t:** Robert Capece/McGraw-Hill, **14bl:** Wally McNamee/Woodfin Camp, **14br:** Michael & Barbara Reed/Animals, Animals; **15:** Ken Lax/McGraw-Hill; **17t:** Burpee Seed, **17c:** W. H. Hodge/Peter Arnold, Inc., **17b:** Ken Lax/McGraw-Hill;

18: Grant Heilman Photography; **20L:** David Overcash/BruceColeman, Inc., **20r:** W. E. Ruth/Bruce Coleman, Inc.; **21L:** Grant Heilman Photography, **21r:** Runk/Schoenberger/Grant Heilman Photography; **22t:** USDA, **22b:** Grant Heilman Photography; **24:** Barry L. Runk/Grant Heilman Photography; **25:** Robert Capece/McGraw-Hill; **26:** Clyde H. Smith/Peter Arnold, Inc.; **28:** Anita Sabarese; **29:** Peter Arnold, Inc.; **30:** Robert Capece/McGraw-Hill; **31tl:** Earth Scenes, **31tr:** Lisa Limer, **31cl:** Lisa Limter, **31cr:** Anita Saberese, **31bl:** Grant Heilman Photography, **31br:** Alan Pitcairn/Grant Heilman Photography

32: R. V. Boger Photo Researchers; **34:** William Harlow; **35:** Grant Heilman Photography; **36:** Grant Heilman Photography; **37:** Peter Vadnai/Mc-Graw-Hill; **38:** Randy Matusow/McGraw-Hill; H. Sund/Image Bank

40: Robert Capece/McGraw-Hill; **42–44:** Peter Vadnai/McGraw-Hill; **45:** Yoav Levy; **46:** Peter Vadnai/McGraw-Hill; **47:** Robert Capece/McGraw-Hill; **48:** Elisabeth Weiland/Photo Researchers; **50t:** Russ Kinne/Photo Researchers; **50b:** Leonard Lee Rue III/Photo Researchers; **51c:** Leonard Lee Rue III, **51b:** American Museum of Natural History; **52t:** John MacGregor/Peter Arnold, Inc., **52c:** Charlie Ott/Photo Researchers; **52b:** Sam Brooks/Photo Researchers; **53tl:** Hal Harrison/Grant Heilman Photography, **53bl:** Hal Harrison/Grant Heilman Photography, **53r:** G. Ziesler/Peter Arnold, Inc.; **54t:** Joseph Van Wormer/Bruce Coleman, **54b:** Leonard Lee Rue III/Monkmeyer; **55t:** Leonard Lee Rue III/Monkmeyer; **55c:** Bruce Coleman, Inc., **55b:** Evelyn Appel;

56: Luis Villota/Image Bank; **58:** Bob Evans/Peter Arnold, Inc.; **59t:** Jeff Rotman/Peter Arnold, Inc., **55b:** Tom McHugh/Photo Researchers; **60t:** Richard Ellis/Photo Researchers, **60b:** Tom McHugh/Photo Researchers; **61:** Russ Kinne/Photo Researchers; **63:** Fred Bavendam/Peter Arnold, Inc.;

64: Leonard Lee Rue III/Photo Researchers; **66tl&br:** Roger Maserang, **66tr:** Tom McHugh/Photo Researchers, **66bl:** Evelyn Appel; **68tl:** Alan Mercer/Stock, Boston; **68tr:** Randy Matusow/McGraw-Hill; **68b:** Morton Beebe/Image Bank; **69:** Robert Capece/McGraw-Hill; **70t:** C. Allan Morgan/Peter Arnold, Inc., **70c:** Peter S. Thacher/Photo Researchers; **70b:** Jeanne White Ottawa/Photo Researchers; **72:** New York Zoological Society; **74:** Ginger Chih/Peter Arnold, Inc.; **75&76:** Robert Capece/McGraw-Hill; **77:** Bill Gillette/Stock, Boston; **78:** Robert Capece/McGraw-Hill;

80: Hugh Rogers/Monkmeyer; **82:** Runk/Schoenberger/Grant Heilman Photography; **83:** Frank Siteman/Stock, Boston; **85t:** Robert Capece/McGraw-Hill; **85b:** John Lei/Stock, Boston; **86t:** Elizabeth Crews/Stock, Boston; **86b:** Peter Vadnai/McGraw-Hill;

88: Robert Capece/McGraw-Hill; **92&93:** Robert Capece/McGraw-Hill; **96&97:** Frank Siteman/Stock, Boston;

98: Photo Researchers; **100:** Peter Vadnai/McGraw-Hill; **102:** Gary Wolinsky/Stock, Boston; **103:** John Colwell/Grant Heilman Photography; **105:** Robert Capece/McGraw-Hill;

106: David Hamilton/Image Bank; **108&110:** Peter Vadnai/McGraw-Hill; **111:** Randy Matusow/McGraw-Hill; **113:** Mark Mittelman/Taurus Photos;